W9-CQM-480

THE STORY OF

EDVARD MUNCH

TOLD TO YOUNG PEOPLE

MARIT LANDE

THE STORY OF EDVARD MUNCH TOLD TO YOUNG PEOPLE

LÆSE selskabet

Marit Lande
'The Story of Edvard Munch –
told to young People'

Publisher:

Illustrated by Edvard Munch

Printed in Norway by
PDC/Norbok AS, Oslo/Gjøvik.

Production:
Ekås Grafisk/Multigraph AS, Oslo

ISBN 82-74430271

FOREWORD

This is a book about Edvard Munch for children and young people.

The sources for much of the text used in this book are Edvard Munch's letters to his family, his journals and his so-called literary notebooks.

With a few exceptions Munch's notes have been incorporated into the text without the use of quotation marks. My aim has been to arouse interest in Edvard Munch as artist and as human being, and my hope to stimulate a deeper interest in his paintings.

Marit Lande

CONTENTS:

1. Edvard Munch´s house and studio at Ekely.

2. The old Edvard Munch at Ekely.

3. Starry Night.
Painting ca. 1923.

During the last years of his life Edvard Munch lived alone in a large house at Ekely, just outside Oslo. There were many rooms in the house, and a large glass verandah – and there were pictures everywhere. They were strewn across the floors, piled against the walls and stacked up against the few items of furniture he had in the house. Even if he walked in his sleep he would know exactly where each picture was. It was best that way, because when someone came to tidy up they always left things in a mess, and he never knew where anything was afterwards.

There was a big, overgrown garden surrounding the house, with apple trees, berry bushes and a lot of scrub. He used to hang his pictures up to dry in the trees, because he thought the fresh air did them good. Beyond the garden was a wide open expanse of land surrounded by rolling hills.

From his verandah Munch could see both the city and the fjord in the south. On dark winter nights the city lights twinkled far off, and the great starry bowl of the night settled across the landscape.

4. Self-portrait: The Night Wanderer. Painting ca. 1930.

When he couldn't sleep at night he used to wander about in his big house. He might stop a while in the bedroom and stand, a little bit shyly, between the bed and the big grandfather clock. On the walls hung those special pictures he always had to have around him – one of them was the figure of a woman with her head bowed sadly down – Eccelesia, he used to call her. When he felt old and tired he would close his eyes and let the thoughts stream through his head. Then the memories of what he'd done and seen long ago would come flooding back, as though it were only yesterday.

He had drawn and painted these memories, as they presented themselves to his inner eye. Through his paintings he had tried to find out the meaning of life, and at the same time to help other people to understand their own lives.

5. Self-portrait between the clock and the bed. Painting ca. 1940.

6. Edvard Munch in his studio at Ekely, on his 75 anniversery.

7. The Dead Mother and the Child. Detail of painting 1897/99.

CHILDHOOD MEMORIES

8. At the gate. Painting ca. 1891.

9. Edvard Munch, 1 year old, on his mother's lap.

10. Edvard Munch, 2 years old.

When Edvard Munch was 4 years old something happened that he was to remember for the rest of his life. The family were living in Lower Castle Street at the time, in Kristiania, which was what Oslo was called in those days. They had moved there a few years earlier from their home at Engelhaug in Løten, because Munch's father worked as an army doctor at Akershus Fortress.

Edvard was going a walk with his mother. They went down some dark stairs and he took his mother by the hand and tugged her along – he couldn't get out fast enough. Down in the street they were nearly blinded by the sharp spring light, and the grass shot up between the cobblestones and shone a brilliant green. His mother had on her black silk dress and a short cape. Her hat was blue, with a ribbon which waved in the wind and hit her in the face. She walked so slowly, kept stopping all the time and breathed heavily. Together they walked down Castle Street towards the fortress and looked at the sea.

11. At the bedside. Litograph 1916.

Not long after this the family moved to Pile Street. The house was close to the Royal Hospital, which had just been built. There were open fields round about. One day when Edvard was playing on the pavement outside the house, some blind people came by. They held onto each other and fumbled their way down the street. The sight moved him powerfully, and straight-away he felt he must draw what he had seen. He didn't have pencil and paper with him so he ran inside, grabbed up a piece of coal and quickly did a drawing of the blind people on the kitchen floor. For a long time afterwards he continued to feel the warm glow of pleasure it had given him to draw like this.

12. Laura Munch with her five children. Left: Sophie and Andreas. Right: Edvard and Laura. Inger on her lap.

There were dark memories too. His mother standing tall and sombre in the bedroom, her hair flowing loose about her shoulders as she leant exhausted against the bed. Edvard and his big sister Sophie sat close together in their little chairs and listened as their mother told them in a quiet voice that soon she would be leaving them. Would Edvard and Sofie be upset when she was gone? They must promise to believe in Jesus, and then they would all be together again one day in heaven.The children didn't really understand, but everything seemed so terribly sad they just began to cry and cry.

He had another very clear memory, from just before Christmas, in the living room in Pile Street. The Christmas tree was covered in white candles up to the top. Some were dripping, and the white candles shone and twinkled, but not as much as the red and yellow and green ones. There was so much light you could hardly see.

Their mother sat in the middle of the sofa, still and pale in her long black silk dress. Her five children stood round her, Sofie, Edvard, Andreas, Inger and Laura. Father paced up and down the room and then sat down beside mother on the sofa. They leant close to each other and whispered something. Everything was so still and so bright.

Mother died soon afterwards. On the night it happened the children were woken up, and one after the other they had to go to her bed. She looked at them in a such a funny way and then she kissed them. A strange man in black stood praying by the bed. It was murky in the room, the air was heavy and grey. Then the children were taken away to a place where they were given cakes and could play as much as they liked. After a long while their father came to take them home. 'Mama is in heaven now', he said. They were so nice to them all, and patted them on their cheeks, but they cried even more. Then Sophie was given a doll, and Edvard a Noah's Ark, and then the crying stopped. When they arrived home, the two big beds were covered up, and everything seemed to huge and barren. Edvard crawled under the bed, looked in the corner. Mama was nowhere.

To Edvard it was as though he and Sofie were all alone in the world. Their brothers and sisters were too small to understand what had happened, and their father's grief was so great that he couldn't seem to get over it.

13. The Dead Mother and the Child. Painting 1897/99.

14. Karen Bjølstad, Edvard's Aunt. Painting 1888.

THE FAMILY AT HOME

After the death of his mother came a great emptiness. His father was silent, and full of melancholy, and he would sit alone for hours on end thinking to himself or else reading the Bible and praying to God.

Often he read to the children the mothers farewell letter to the family: 'Jesus Christ will make you happy here and in the hereafter; love Him above all things, and do not grieve Him by turning your backs to Him; often I am filled with fear that in Heaven I might not see some of you who are my heart's delight here on earth again, but with faith in the Lord who has promised to hear our prayers, so long as the Lord still grants me life, I shall beseech Him to save your souls. And now, my beloved children, my dear, sweet ones, I say farewell to you. Your beloved Papa will better teach you the way to Heaven. I shall be waiting for all of you there. God be with you now and forever, Sophie, pale little Edvard, Andreas and Laura and you, my dear, sweet unforgettable, self-sacrificing husband.'

Then Aunt Karen came. She was his mother's sister and became almost like a real mother to the five children. Edvard remembered her best sitting in a rocking-chair, usually with

15. Siesta. Painting 1883.

16. Aunt Karen in her Rocking Chair. Painting 1883.

a piece of sewing or knitting. There were always clothes that needed mending, and it was important to try to get the clothes to last as long as possible.

Aunt Karen was also an artist, she drew and painted water-colours and she could make the most beautiful little pictures out of moss and leaves. She sold these to the craft shop, and used the money she got to help towards the housekeeping.

17. Dr. Munch´s home office. Watercolour 1875.

When Edvard was 12 the family moved to Grünerløkka on the other side of the river Aker. This was a new development, people called it 'best east-end'. Craftsmen and workers who had recently moved in from the country used to live here, mostly people who were not very well off. Family friends and relations lived on the other side of town, a long way away, so there were less visits than before.

The father, Christian Munch had a large family to keep, and there wasn't a lot of money to go round – in fact, often there was barely enough. He had a modest income as an army doctor, and by moving to this new area he had hoped to get some more patients and earn a bit more money. The patients came alright, the only trouble was they often didn't have enough to pay for their treatment. But Dr Munch worked hard.

He had a surgery at home in a room that was partitioned off by a curtain that hung from the ceiling, and there he saw the patients who were well enough to go out;but more often than not he had to visit his patients in their own homes. It never occurred to him to say no when a message came asking him to call.

Edvard recalled one occasion when he went with his father to see a sick boy all the way over in the suburb Kampen. It was twilight when they left and completely dark by the time they arrived. The house was tiny, with just one room, and just one bed inside that room. A boy lay dozing in the bed, and a large fat rat suddenly raced across the floor.

18. Dr. Christian Munch. Painting 1885.

19. Afternoon at Olaf Ryes Square. Painting 1883.

There was a lot of sickness in Grünerløkka. It was almost as though people got ill because of the houses they lived in, big dark tenement halls with 3 or 4 floors. People moved into them even before the plaster was properly dry. You could feel the cold in the big entries, in the dark stairwells and in the flats themselves where the walls seemed to give off a raw damp. It was only warm and cheerful round the woodstoves. In winter the snow piled up like an icy wall along the river bank and seemed to hold the whole of the area in a freezing grip.

But how different everything was in summer, when the chestnut and the fruit trees blossomed in Grüners garden, and Aunt Karen planted flowers in the little garden in front of their building. Olaf Ryes Square was like an oasis of green in among all the sad grey houses, and on Sundays people picniced there while the children played.

Father used to sit in a corner of the sofa near the stove, half-hidden behind a bluey haze of tobacco smoke as the sun reflected across his grey hair. He seemed so remote. When he wasn't busy seeing patients he was usually buried in a book, or he lay and rested on the sofa.

But now and then he would take down one of his big thick books and read to the children, something from 'Stories of the ancient gods and heroes of the North', or fairy tales or ghost stories. These were special occasions for the children.

The children sat quite still and listened. Father would get carried away by what he was reading, and for a while the everyday world with its sickness and its money-problems would disappear. Then a whole new world seemed to open up, full of strange and exciting beings and adventures.

20. Dr. Christian Munch on the Sofa. Painting 1881.

21. The Death of Earl Håkon. Watercolour 1877.

22. Polli, Sophie´s Finch. Watercolour 1875.

While father read, the children sat round the table drawing. The stories fired their imagination, they could see them as though they were really happening.

When father read from the history book, the death of Earl Hakon was as real to them as Sofie's pet finch Polli. But for someone who liked to draw it was never difficult to find a subject. Medicine jars, father's pipe, the furniture in the room – anything was worth drawing, and taking a lot of care to get right.

23. The Living Room at Number 48 Thorvald Meyers Street. Drawing 1875.

24. Copy of the painting "Bridal Procession in Hardanger", by Tidemand og Gude. Watercolour 1875.

25–29 Drawings 1875–80.

E. Münch. 1877.

The medicine jar was part of their everyday life. Sickness was too. Edvard was a frail child, and when he was 13 he coughed up blood and was very ill. He clasped his hands together and prayed to God not to let him die, and his father prayed with him: 'Lord help him if it be your will – do not let him die. . .' The others stood round the bed, some red-faced from weeping, others pale – and he seemed to see other faces in the room. . . Outside the church bells rang in Christmas Day. Then everything went white. And when he woke again he saw his father's smiling face leaning over him.

With the coming of spring Edvard slowly got better. The first rays of the sun struck the west-facing wall, shining through the windows and glinting on the golden frames of the family portraits and the shiny red cupboard in his room. He sat by the window in the sunlight and drew.

30. Edvard Medicine Jar and Spoon. Watercolour 1877.

31. At the Death Bed. Lithograph 1897.

32. The Son. Woodcut 1920.

*33. Old Aker Church
Drawings 1877.*

At that time the family were living in Foss Way in Grünerløkka. From the windows they could see the cupola of the Trinity Church. In the churchyard below one could imagine to see right to the family grave, where mother and Sophie were buried. They also had a fine view across the river Aker to where Old Aker Church stood so majestically on a hilltop. On Sunday mornings the church bells of Old Aker Church sounded so solemnly.

On the road leading up to it which he had so often walked with his father on Sundays was a row of tightly-packed little wooden houses. Over and over again he painted the view of the church from his window, not giving up until he was completely satisfied with the result.

Inside the church with its thick walls was so lovely. As he watched his father kneel to receive the sacrament he thought of all the people who had come to mass in this church over the centuries. He painted a rosary and thought of all the prayers that had been prayed, and he painted the chalice and the crucifixion as he thought of his father and of his father's faith in God.

34. Old Aker Church. Drawing 1875.

35. Father at prayer. Woodcut 1902.

The God of his father was a stern God. He had often argued with his father about this. He could not accept, as his father did, that the unbelievers should be condemned to be tortured in hell for a thousand years. Surely God could not be as cruel as that. . . The argument ended with him leaving in a temper and slamming the door after him. But after wandering in the streets for a while he calmed down again and went back home to make it up with his father. He opened the door very quietly and saw that his father was kneeling in prayer by the bed. The candle by his bed cast a yellow light across his nightshirt. He went to his own room, but he was restless and unable to sleep. In the end he got out his drawing pad and did a drawing of his father as he had seen him. Finally he was satisfied, and then he lay down and was soon asleep.

Then Sofie fell ill. She'd been troubled by a cough for a long time, and red patches appeared in her cheeks. 'Keep away from draughts', the doctor told her when Sofie went out with her friends and spent hours hanging around the street corners. And one evening she lay flushed and feverish in bed. Her eyes were bright and her gaze flickered around the room. She spat blood and began hallucinating.

The priest came in his dark habit. He went into the sick-room and the door was closed behind him. Sofie tried to get up. She pointed to the wicker chair standing by the bed. They lifted her up carefully and sat her in the chair, put a pillow behind her head and a thick rug over her lap. 'I want so much to live', she whispered. 'It's so nice here. . .'

The family stood around as she died – like stones. Everything was quite still.

36. Death in the Sickroom. Painting 1893.

37. From Maridalen. Painting 1881.

And then, gradually, life moved on again – without Sofie. Edvard had missed a lot of schooling because of his illness, and now he made his mind up he would study at home. Twice a week a friend of the family came to teach him maths, and he studied other subjects with his father. In the evenings there was drawing and reading aloud.

Only rarely was the quiet rhythm of family life disturbed by visits from friends and relatives. On Sundays, after church, he went to the Artist's Society or to the National Gallery and studied the collections there.

But in the summer, when the weather was fine, he and his brothers and sisters went walking to Maridalen valley or Bogstad Water. On such occasions they made an early start and were often up with the sun at 4 in the morning – walking all way it was important to make the most of the day.

Birthdays were special days in the family, and Edvard always remembered his 15th birthday in particular. His father gave him 2 kroner, his Aunt Karen a pair of woollen gloves and from

Andreas, Laura and Inger he got a pound of brazil nuts. For the meal there was steak and red pudding, and in the evening they played cards for the brazil nuts.

Later on he was measured – it was a birthday tradition. He stood upright against the wall and his father ceremoniously placed a ruler across his head and made a little mark on the wall behind him. He was then 1 meter and 54 cm tall, and was beginning to feel that he was growing into a man.

38. Edvard Munch , aged about 15.

In the summer Edvard was allowed to go with his father to the military camp at Helgelandsmoen, where Dr Munch was working then. In June he took the train up to Ringerike.

The journey was an experience in itself, and he thoroughly enjoyed the beautiful landscape round Tyrifjord, where flat, lush islands lay and floated on the mirror-still surface of the water. He and his father went for long walks. Sometime they walked until midnight without getting tired. The blonde summer night were so beatiful that they did not dear to speak – the moon shedding gold over the landscape. They visited the priest in Hole, who offered them home-made beer and strawberries and cream.

On midsummer's eve he was allowed to join the grown-ups party with his father. He had his best suit and his summer hat sent from Kristiania, and when he asked the young ladies to dance he thought it was a wonderful thing to be grown-up.

39. The Sick-bay at Helgelandsmoen. Painting 1882.

40. The Sick-bay at Gardermoen. Watercolour 1879.

All the time he worked regularly at his drawing and his water-colours. He drew the old rectory and Norderhov Church, and painted water-colours of the views. At military camp Gardermoen he drew the sick-bay and the surgery, and took great care to ensure that his drawings were accurate and showed the buildings just as they really were. His father was very proud of his work. He showed his drawings to his collegues and relations, and really enjoyed their admiration.

Drawing was no longer just a hobby for him. A young man in his 16th year also needs to begin thinking about what job he's going to do. His father thought the most sensible idea was for him to attend the Technical School, so that he could train to be an architect or an engineer. Before they could be admitted to the school pupils had to submit drawings to see if they were good enough, so this was one very good reason for taking the work so seriously.

Edvard followed his father's advice and began at the school – it was the autumn before he turned 16. The school was a pleasant place and he liked his fellow-pupils, and in the common-room they had enjoyable discussions and uproarious parties. But all the time he was aware that there was something much more important – something he HAD to do: he had to paint pictures.

41. Upper Foss Farm. Painting 1880.

42. The main building at Upper Foss Farm. Drawing 1879.

He got himself brushes and oils so that he could begin oil painting. He went off one day to paint Upper Foss Farm, a lovely old building down by the river Aker, not far from where they lived in Foss Way. He was quite proud of this first oil painting of his.

43. Old Aker Church. Painting 1881.

STUDENT YEARS IN KRISTIANIA

In the autumn Edvard made up his mind. 'My decision is now that I will become a painter' he wrote with great formality in his diary. He knew that his future would be difficult and uncertain, and that his father would be upset. But he knew too that he really didn't have any choice. He was almost 18 years old.

Once he had made up his mind he set to work with a venegance. He made himself an easel so that he could paint outdoors, and from the University he obtained prints of works by well-known painters which he practiced copying.

Soon he had his first commission. It came from his great-aunts in Pile Street who wanted a painting of their living-room. From his many visits there he was already thoroughly familiar with the room – he and his brothers and sisters had often taken a nap on the green biedermeyer with the rug neatly folded over the arm.

Their gold-framed great-grandparents on the wall behind them stared down on them so forbiddingly that they instinctively sat up straighter – and the minutes crept by as they waited for the cuckoo in the clock to show himself.

He visited his aunts five times in the course of the painting, to ensure that the finished product was as exact and true as possible. His aunts were very pleased with it, and as a reward he was given a large cup of drinking chocolate and a beautiful drawing pad.

44. The Aunts Sitting Room. Painting 1881.

45. A street in Kristiania. Drawing ca. 1884.

It soon became clear that it would be no easy matter to make a living as a painter. A few months later he sent three small pictures to be auctioned at a gallery. Most of what was sold went for a price that hardly covered the cost of the frame, and Edvard himself even had to buy one of his own pictures back. For the other two he got 11 crowns and 15,50 crowns – very modest sums of money even in those days. For a while he tried to sell his drawings to the illustrated magazines. One called the Norwegian Family Magazine was quite willing to use the drawings, but all the fee they could offer was a free copy of the magazine.

That same autumn Edvard began attending evening classes at the Drawing School, and his art studies began in earnest. The instruction there was systematic and thorough. First the pupils had to learn to draw figures as blocks and geometrical forms. Edvard found this rather boring, because this was what he had already done for a long time at home. He therefore was allowed to by-pass these classes and go straight to the top class where the students did figure studies with a life-model.

46. Self-portrait. Painting 1881.

His first teacher at the Drawing School was the sculptor Julius Middelthun, a dignified, handsome, elderly man who would not stand for any nonsense in the classroom. Once when a student added a landscape behind one of the naked figures he grew almost angry – the idea here was to draw from life – nothing more and nothing less.

Christian Krohg was a different type altogether. The following year Munch and a number of other young painters rented a studio in town so that they could work together and learn from one another. Krohg was the most famous painter in Kristiania at the time, and when he offered his services as teacher, absolutely free, it was impossible to refuse. When Krohg arrived he almost filled the place with his four-square figure and his huge beard. He flew through the studio like a storm, making corrections here and there on his 'pupils' pictures where he thought it was called for.

Later Edvard Munch realised that he had probably learnt just as much from old Middelthun who had shown him how to model on canvas. And it was Middelthun's advice he followed when he sat in front of the mirror and painted one of his first self-portraits.

47. The Living Room in Foss Way. Drawing 1877.

48. From Hakloa in Nordmarka. Drawing ca. 1882.

The following year he exhibited for the first time. At the Artist Autumn Show he introduced himself to the public for the first time with a portrait of a young woman – 'Study of a head' he called the picture. There was a tense wait for the critics reaction: the model had small eyes, and she was ugly, wrote Dagbladet – but it was realistic and well-painted. He had been accepted.

One of Munch's friends at this time was a man named Frits Thaulow. Thaulow was a painter too. He had been to Paris and came back bursting with new ideas which caused a flurry in the art world.

Thaulow was the one who arranged exhibitions and the one who persuaded the painters to leave their dusty and artificially lit garrets and start working outside from nature. Only then is art real and genuine, said Thaulow. He knew of the ideal place for them – an estate near Modum Dyeworks. A whole crowd of them travelled there in the summer to live and work together.

It was marvellous to be out in the country, where the air was clean and the nature beautiful, and Munch jumped at the chance. But he had already been painting directly from nature for a long

49. Morning. Painting 1884

time. He and his friends had sat out for hours painting in a boat on the river Aker, and he had many pictures from the Nordmarka and Maridalen which had all been painted direct from nature.

He knew it was time to move on. He saw the sunlight streaming in through a white curtain, and saw how the light changed everything it touched.

At Modum he found a model, a young girl from one of the neighbouring estates, and painted her as she sat on the edge of the bed in the morning sunlight in the act of putting on her stockings. The light turned the everyday subject into poetry – and almost everything in the picture was light and white.

The same autumn the picture was entered for the Autumn Show and again Munch waited tensely for the critics judgement.

But this time, according to the newspapers, everything was wrong. It was wrong to paint a mere servant girl – for she was obviously no refined lady – nor was it properly and clearly painted like the other paintings in the exhibition.

Edvard Munch wandered round the exhibition and looked at all the pretty, prim pictures, all of them painted as clearly as any photograph. And it seemed to him that there had to be more to painting than simply reproducing exact copies of reality. In any case, how could one compete with nature itself?

He knew that what the eye sees depends very much on the mood one is in – things in the morning look different to things in the evening, and perception changes according to whether one is happy or sad. How often he had had direct, personal experience of this, as on that bright spring day when the brass band came marching down Karl Johan's Street, filling him with happiness, and the spring and the light and the music melted together into a quivering ecstasy. The music 'charged' the colours, and when he later came to paint this picture he tried to get an effect of the colours shimmering in time to the music.

50. Approach of the marching Band at Karl Johan. Painting 1889.

51. Self portrait with a Sceleton arm. Lithograph 1895.

Moreover, as he well knew, real art is something that emerges from human life, from joys and sorrows. But most of all from sorrows. He felt that humans' fate is like that of planets that move in space and cross each other's orbits; a pair of stars that is fated to meet strays towards one another only for a moment, then each disappears to its own region in the vastness of space. And he knew deep inside himself that no matter what others might think he would have to paint things the way he saw them with his inner eye.

The sight of Sofie's pale face against the white pillow had etched itself across his mind forever. Nor would he ever forget the

52. The Sick Child. Painting 1896.

grief he felt the time he looked at her and her image became a little blurred because of the tears in his eyes. It was this earliest of memories he wanted to paint, the sight of her just before she died, when she had seemed almost translucent. But as soon as he started work it was as though this first impression of her had vanished, he had to scrape over the picture and start anew, and then again, over and over again. He thinned the paint so that it trickled down the canvas and in this way managed to reproduce the effect of his tears. When he was finally finished, he knew that no one had ever before painted a picture quite like this. He knew also that from now on there was no way back for him: from now on he would

53. The Sick Child. Drypoint 1894.

have to paint his own feelings, his own joys and sorrows so that others too would be able to share in them.

The picture was submitted for exhibition, and he didn't really expect anyone else to understand it but himself. He was the only one, after all, who had experienced Sofie's death, and he alone had felt the grief. All the same it was strange to see how people crowded round the picture, some shouting and screaming, some furiously angry.

Angriest of all was Gustav Wentzel. 'A phoney painter', he shrieked. Wentzel was a painter too, the type who did the kinds of paintings people like to hang up over the sofa. He painted so

54. Christiania Bohemia. Etching 1895.

realistically that one could see every last little object in the picture, every nail in the floor, every knot in the woodwork. But, thought Edvard Munch, we can'tall be nail-and-knot painters.

Fortunately there were a few – a very few – who did understand his paintings. One was Hans Jaeger. Jaeger had written a book called 'Among the Kristiania Bohemians', where the plot and all the characters were taken from his own circle of friends and acquaintances. The book was about a little group of artists living in Kristiania who didn't want to live and think like everybody else. They despised polite society, hated God and the church and next after them hated the idea of family and marriage. 'You shall break from your family' was one of their 'commandments'.

Edvard Munch portrayed Jaeger in the Grand Café on Karl Johan's Street, where he used to sit and watch people passing by on the pavement – and where they could see and notice him too. Jaeger and his friends could sit for hours at the café table drinking and smoking, talking and arguing about things. They held wild parties too.

Edvard Munch sat and listened to these discussions. He didn't say much himself, but he thought a lot. He thought that in among all the talk and the drinking, from these lonely people in their sad cafés he was hearing ideas and thoughts that he would later be able to make use of in his own paintings. 'You must write your own life' said Jaeger. And Munch too began to write down notes and impressions which, many years later, he turned into paintings and drawings.

But all the time he could see his father's sad eyes on him, and he knew how much he suffered. For his father the bohemians circle and everything it stood for was something evil and dangerous that was threatening to take his son away from him.

Munch thought often of an occasion when his father came home from his travels. He wanted to make peace between them and take a glass of wine together, but Edvard had just answered 'No thanks', in a careless way. How much he wished he could put his arms around him, not once but many times, and tell him how much he loved him. . .

55. The Morning after. Painting 1894.

56. Anxiety. Lithograph 1896.

57. Evening on Karl Johan. Painting 1893/94.

Often, when he emerged from the Grand Café onto Karl Johan, Edvard felt a strange depression. Later he remembered one occasion in particular. It was in the evening and the sun was setting behind the castle, throwing the contours of its silhouette into sharp relief against the clear air. And there stood the Parliament building shining like gold against the dark blue sky.

People in dark winter clothes streamed along the pavement towards him. Everybody who passed by looked at him, stared at him, all those faces, pallid in the evening light. He tried to consentrate on some thought, but he could not. All he felt was emptiness in his head.

And then it was as though everything became so silent. The noise from the street became so distant, seemed to come from above. He no longer had any sensation in his leg, his whole body trembled, and sweat ran down him. He felt that he was able to see behind everyone's masks. Peacefully smiling faces, pale corpses who endlessly sent their tortuous way down the road that seemed to lead to a grave. . .

In his diary he noted down carefully the details of this experience. Later he painted 'Evening on Karl Johan', depicting the passing people with stiff, empty faces.

58. Edvard Munch, at the age of 27.

At the age of 26 Munch organised his first one-man show. He wanted to exhibit everything he had done so far, from the first efforts to his latest work. People in Kristiania were astonished: had he no modesty, young Munch? Was he incapable of self-criticism? No painter before him had had the nerve to put on an exhibition devoted entirely to his own works. But others understood that here was an artist with a unique talent – and as a result of the exhibition he was given a scholarship to travel to Paris and study.

59. Self Portrait with brushes. Painting 1904.

MUNCH ABROAD

60. View from Munchs room in St. Cloud over the Seine. Painting 1890.

A grey autumn day he left Kristiania to go to France. Paris was an experience. From the long, gloomy autumn evenings at home, Munch came to a world that was brilliantly lit by countless electric lights in the evenings. From the balcony of his hotel he could look down on a street teeming with life. People walked arm in arm in the sunlight, horses and wagons rolled by with a deafening clatter. According to his calendar it was October, but for Munch it was as though it was the beginning of spring.

He began at the art school, where were life-drawing classes. It was all really pretty much the same as back home, and soon it began to bore him: how many times does the head fit into the body, how broad is the chest compared to the length of the body, and so on. . .

But when classes finished for the morning he had the whole of the long afternoon to do what he liked. And there was so much to see. People flocked into Paris to see the new Eiffel Tower, a fantastic steel construction that was the tallest building ever raised in that part of the world.

Edvard Munch, however, had little time for such diversions. It was the art galleries and the museums that attracted him. And here, in the pictures he saw, it was as though he met his own ideas and thoughts – in various ways, painters had tried to depict nature through the filter of an individual mood, a private awareness.

61. Rue Lafayette. Painting 1891.

62. Night. Painting 1891.

The winter in Paris that year was raw and cold. There was an epidemic of influenza, many people died and there was always a funeral procession passing along the street. The air was cleaner outside the city, so Munch moved to one of the suburbs where he rented a pleasant room above a café.

63. From a Café in St. Cloud. Drawing 1891.

It was a relief to get away from artistic circles in Paris. Most of those who lived in the suburbs were ordinary workers, and in the evenings Munch could sit in the café and talk with them, and with Madame who owned the place. This was how he picked up most of his French. From his room he had a view over the Seine, where the steamships passed on their way to and from Paris. And on a nearby hill was a lovely park with ruins in it, where he used to sit and look out over the city. It was so peaceful up there. All you could hear was the faint sighing that rose up from the huge city with its thousands of roofs and steeples and factory chimneys. The church domes shone like gold and smoke rose into the air from the factories and the railways. In the evenings he would often sit at his window and look out across the river where the steamboat glided by with its red and green lights. The moon shone in through the window and shadowed the cross-pieces into the form of a crucifix on the floor.

One day he received news that his father was dead. He thought of his father the time when they had said goodbye to each other on the quayside. Both of them were a bit shy, neither one really wanted to reveal how much the parting upset them. And he thought of his Aunt Karen and his brother and sisters at home – how would they manage now?

64. Promenade des Anglais in Nice. Painting 1891/92

The winter turned even colder – Edvard Munch had never been so cold in his life. The little coal-oven in the room didn't give of much heat, and after lying in bed with a rheumatic fever for many days he made up his mind that he would travel south – to the Mediterranean. So one day in early January he boarded a train, well-wrapped up in his feather-quilt and with a bottle of wine to keep his spirits up on the journey.

The Mediterranean was a revelation – like a tale from the thousand and one nights. He settled in Nice, where there were roses in the gardens and oranges on the trees. The market-place was like a single enormous flower-bed. And the blue sea beyond, just a shade deeper than the sky, with the long waves breaking gently against the sand. . .

It was as warm as June, and along the Promenade people strolled in their new spring clothes, shaded from the midday sun beneath gaily coloured parasols. Here were pale Parisiennes with their tiny lap-dogs, and young men with trousers as wide as sacks, as well as hollow-chested tuberculosis patients from all over the world.

65. Beneath the Palms in Nice. Painting 1891/92.

Money was now his only problem. The stipend had just about run out, and he hadn't even enough to go along to the barber for a haircut. It was all very humiliating. He didn't like to ask for money from home, where Inger earned a little from giving piano lessons and Aunt Karen from the pictures she sold to the craft shop, just enough for them to get along. But there was another way to make money – a way both dangerous and tempting.

Not far from Nice was Monte Carlo, with its casinos and roulette wheels. It was possible to gamble and win huge sums of money there – if one was lucky. But it was also possible to lose everything one had. The casinos exerted a magnetic attraction on him, and Edvard Munch felt he had to try his luck – it was only a short ride away on the train. As he journeyed he was only vaguely aware of the lovely scenery the train passed through. He was just not interested in it.

The casino, on the other hand, was like some enchanted castle, where the demons of the world assembled for their conventions. There were Indian princes and Russian aristocrats, and office-workers from the provinces, all entertaining the same hope – of winning undreamt of riches.

In the great halls people packed tightly around the roulette tables and waited breathless with excitement for the wheel to stop spinning. The intense green of the tables had the effect of making the surrounding faces glow red – and they seemed twisted with tension.

Edvard Munch followed the play closely and jotted down notes in a small notebook. He tried to work out a system of his own – he needed money to carry on working, after all, and with luck maybe he could win some here. . .

66. At the Roulette Table. Painting 1892.

67. Despair. Drawing 1891.

But he quickly found out that it wasn't safe for him to remain, for the place seemed to cast a spell over him. An inexplicable anxiety overcame him, and in the grip of this strange mood made his way back to his lodgings.

Back in Nice Edvard Munch continued to note down memories of experiences that had made a particular impression on him. He was often thinking of a walk with two friends back in Kristiania, on a hill overlooking the fjord, and then he wrote:

'I was walking along the path with two friends the sun went down – suddenly the sky turned a bloody red – I stopped, leaned against a balustrade, utterly exhausted – saw the blazing clouds like blood and swords – the blue-black fjord and the city – my friends carried on walking – I stood there shaking with fear – I felt like a single huge endless scream through nature.'

He knew he must paint this fear, exactly as he had experienced it that day. He drew the figure of a man wearing a hat and coat, leaning against a fence and looking down the Kristiania fjord.

68. The Scream. Litograph 1893.

But he was not quite satisfied with this painting. It did not fully express his feelings, nor his experience of the sunset he had seen that evening.

For a long time, he had wanted to paint the sunset he remembered. Red like blood. But no one could experience it like he did. This had made him sad and filled him with fear. Sad because the painter's humble means were never sufficient. Still – he wanted to do it – try to paint this fear.

Then he painted 'Scream', and used every means at his disposal to give the fear visible form: he made the figure in the foreground appear to be disintegrating with fear, the lines from the figure flowing out into the wave-like lines of the surrounding nature. And the colours were screams too, red, green and blue-black-screams.

69. The Scream. Painting 1895.

70. The Lonely One. Mezzotint and drypoint on zink. 1896.

71. The Voice. Painting 1893.

It was lovely by the Mediterranean, but Edvard Munch longed to be somewhere else. Back home in Norway, on the west side of the Oslo fjord, is as little town called Åsgårdstrand. He had rented a nice little three-roomed house there, down by the beach. There were lilacs there, and jasmine bushes, and a hammock slung between the trees. And in the house next door lived a pleasant young woman who could come and do the housekeeping and cook the meals.

He wanted to go home in the summer. Nowhere else were the summer nights so lovely. The moon painted a column of gold across the water, and behind lay the great silent pine wood. He often went walking in the evenings along the soft paths, sometimes in the company of a young girl – she was so small she had to stand up on a tussock just to look him in the eye. It was a shame that such love-affairs lasted only a short time – always, after a while, he would feel the same crushing emptiness. No, a bachelor's life was probably the thing for him after all. Love usually only ended up causing jealousy and misery.

72. Melancholy. Painting 1892.

73. From the beach in Åsgårdstrand.

In Åsgårdstrand Munch had seen how his friend Jappe had suffered the pains of love. Jappe grew gloomy and depressed, he often sat and moped on his own. Munch did a painting of him down on the beach among the big round boulders, and made it seem as though the whole of nature echoed Jeppe's despair. He painted his friend's sweetheart as a little white speck in the background, making ready to go off on a boat ride with another man.

74. Self Portrait under a Female mask. Painting 1892.

He knew that his time in France, the pictures he had seen, the people he had met, the books he had read and all his experiences there had made it possible for him to paint everything that has been bottled up inside him for so long. Only now had he found the right pictorial language to be able to make his thoughts visible. He simplified shapes, cut out unnecessary detail, determined to concentrate only on what really mattered. And what really mattered were peoples feelings. He knew that never again would he paint everyday things like people reading or a woman knitting – from now on he would paint people's feelings, their passions, their suffering and love.

It was strange to be back in Kristiania again. Karl Johan during the promenade hour was as lively as it had ever been, and in among the dark winter clothes were bright flashes of colour from some lady's parasol or a light summer dress. But behind the gay facade lurked envy and narrow-mindedness. Edvard Munch had been awarded the State scholar ship for artists, for three years in succession, and a lot of people were annoyed by this. The famous author Bjørnson wrote an article in the newspaper and put the question straight: had Munch simply been on holiday there in the south? Or had he been using the money as a sort of sickness benefit for himself?

Edvard Munch made up his mind to hold an exhibition of all the work he had done while he had been away. It opened in a gallery on Karl John – a big exhibition containing over 50 paintings as well as many drawings and sketches. The reaction was more or less what he had expected. A few painters were enthusiastic, but in the main people didn't like it, and the reviews in the papers were bad.

75. Spring on Karl Johan. Painting 1892.

76. The Kiss. Painting 1892.

Then something extraordinary happened. A Norwegian painter, Adelsten Normann was his name, passed through Kristiania on his way to Berlin. He visited the exhibition and was wildly enthusiastic. Beeing a member of the Berlin Society of Artists, he thought that Edvard Munch's paintings should be somthing for the Berlin artists to see, and he invited Munch to hold an exhibition in Berlin. The exhibition opened that same autumn, in the elegant surroundings of the Berlin Society of Artists.

Now there was a real outcry. People were furious and demanded that the exhibition be closed down at once. The pictures, it was said, were an affront against art. Not a day passed without some comment in the newspapers. It seemed to be mostly the old who disapproved and the young who were in favour.

It was the best publicity imaginable, and Munch was in fact extremely pleased – it was the most amusing time of his life. It was as though a war were about to break out, everyone was making ready to go to battle.

What surprised him most was that something as innocent as painting could be responsible for such passions.

77. Tingel-Tangel. Lithograph 1895.

Almost overnight Munch became famous, the person everyone talked about. He was invited out to balls and for dinners and had to go out and buy himself an evening dress. In the evenings he frequented a little café that was a haunt of artists – it was almost like the bohemian days back in Kristiania. He met the sculptor Gustav Vigeland there, as well as several old friends from Kristiania.

And then there was August Strindberg. Both Munch and Strindberg knew that they were soul-mates, they thought the same thoughts and felt that their two minds vibrated on the same wavelength. Both were preoccupied with literature and psychology, and both painted. The first painting Munch did in Berlin was of the famous Swedish writer. When he came to pose for the painting he would place a pistol on the table, and afterwards he would leave without offering a word of explanation. A strange man, Strindberg. For a time he was very interested in chemical experiments and tried to make gold. And he seemed to have a kind of power over people, even from a distance. Years later, once when Munch was painting on a beach, a gust of wind knocked his easel over. Afterwards he used to tell people that it was Strindberg who had influenced the wind to do it.

Munch did a portrait of Strindberg and wrote his name in the border round the edge of the picture – but with one of the letters missing. STINDBERG, it said on the finished picture. Most peculiar.

78. August Strindberg. Lithograph 1897.

79. Puberty. painting 1893.

80. Madonna. Lithograph. 1895.

Edvard Munch experienced a great damburst of creativity while in Berlin. The work poured out of him – drawings and paintings, pictures that had been stored up inside him for years. What he wanted to do was paint people's feelings, the whole emotional life of a human being. He wanted to paint love, fear and death, so that when all the pictures were put together they would almost be a kind of poem about life itself. Later he gave a name to all these pictures – the Frieze of Life.

He painted a young girl sitting naked on the edge of a bed, her eyes wide and staring. On the wall behind her he put a dark and threatening shadow, and it was as though the girl's fears were made visible by the shadow, and as though he were showing his own fears too.

He painted a woman in the act of love, in the very moment when new life took root in her. And he wrote a caption to the picture: 'Now life reaches out a hand to death. The link is forged in the great chain that joins the ten thousand dead to the ten thousand yet to come. '

81. Madonna. painting 1893.

82. Parting. Painting 1896.

He painted parting, the painful kind that he himself had experienced: a young woman dressed in white walks away, while the man remains suffering where he is. He painted the woman's hair so that it twined round the man's head and reached straight to his heart. And as she moves away the heart bleeds. He thought of the beach in Åsgårdstrand, and he felt that there he could find an image of himself, of his life. The strange smell of seaweed and sea reminded him of a young woman, and in the dark water he could see the color of her eyes.

At the man's feet Munch painted a blood-red bush, and it seemed to him that this is how real art is born – it grows from the blood of a human heart.

While working on these pictures he made the discovery that there really is no clear distinction between love and fear, life and death, that every aspect of a human life is part of the same weave.

Edvard Munch soon found out that it was not easy to keep the public's interest in a big city like Berlin. Strindberg left, and soon the crowd he had joined had split up and its members gone their separate ways. Munch too left and went home to Norway.

Back in Kristiania Munch arranged a large exhibition consisting of all the pictures he had painted while in Berlin.

The reaction from the public was the same – there was a general outcry. Some even called the police and demanded that the gallery be closed. A doctor who specialised in diseases of the mind was of the opinion that Munch's art was abnormal and that he needed treatment.

Henrik Ibsen attended the exhibition, and Munch thought it a great honour to meet the famous writer. 'You'll discover what I discovered' said Ibsen, 'the more enemies you have the more friends you win.' He was particularly interested in one big painting – 'The 3 stages of Woman' – and asked Munch to explain it to him. 'There's the dreaming woman, ' said Munch, 'then the woman in love with life, and then the woman in grief. . . and behind the tree stands a pale-faced man who doesn't understand any of it. . . '

When Ibsen's latest play was about to be performered at the theatre scene in Paris, Munch was asked to do a poster for the play. He made a protrait of Ibsen with his great halo of hair and bushy side-whiskers.

83. The Woman in Three Stages. Painting 1894.

84. Henrik Ibsen at the Grand Café. Painting 1906/10.

85. Henrik Ibsen and Jappe Nilssen in Grand Café. Drawing ca 1930.

The next few years were an intense and restless period. Munch travelled a lot between the capitals and cities of Europe, always living in different hotels and meeting new people. His Aunt Karen and his brother and sisters at home were his anchorage during this restless period.

Karen and Inger were often ill, and they were not very well off. Munch began to sell paintings at about this time and often sent the money straight home. People flocked to his exhibitions and in Germany there was published a book about him.

Edvard Munch knew of a way of making several pictures at once, so that he could sell even more of them. By scraping the subject onto a metal plate he could go back to it later and print as many copies of the picture as he wanted. He began carrying a little copper-plate about with him so that whenever he saw a subject that interested him, he could straightaway do an outline of it on the plate.

It was exhilarating to experiment with new techniques. He also tried drawing with a sort of wax-crayon on a stone-plate and making prints from the stone afterwards.

86. The Sick Child. Lithograph 1896.

This was a more laborious process, because the stones were heavy, but by using different kinds of paper with different colours he achieved some wonderful effects. He made a print of 'The Sick Child' – Sofie's pale face against the white pillow – using several colours, a different one for each stone. He had to get an experienced printer to help him, but he insisted on being in charge of the work himself. He could give his instructions without even looking – yellow, pink, red. . . Then he opened his eyes and said: 'Right, it's time for a glas of schnapps now'. The printer kept on working until Munch came back, and once more, he ordered: 'Yellow, pink, red.' All the time he was thinking of the Frieze of Life, the pictures that would be like a poem about life and love and death.

87. The Kiss. Drypoing and aquatint. 1895.

88. Anxiety. Painting 1894.

Actually the pictures should all be hung together, in Munch's opinion. Preferably in a room of their own where the people who saw them would be able to understand the connection between life and death. He managed to exhibit them like this in Berlin. Ten years after the scandal over his earlier show, the paintings from the Frieze of Life were collected and exhibited in a large hall. Munch called the exhibition 'Pictures from Life', and divided it up into several different sections. One series showed 'the seeds of love', while another dealt with the difficulties of adult love. One section was devoted to fear, and there were many pictures on the subject of death, based on his own experiences of it at home. The exhibition attracted a great deal of attention, and was a huge success. Munch felt it was a great personal triumph.

In Kristiania Munch had met a woman who had quite an influence on his life and his art. Her name was Tulla Larsen, she was a pretty lady at 29, daughter of a rich merchant in Kristiania.

Munch noticed that her face was capable of so many different expressions – she had three expressions, each so striking that it was as though she were three different people. He started work on a new painting, of people dancing by the sea on a summer night, with the moon like a column of gold across the surface of the water.

As he painted the three women, the one in white, the one in red and the one in black, he thought of Tulla, with her fair hair that was like a halo around her face. Tulla was in the middle of the dance of life and she pulled him along with her.

Tulla was always there. Munch went to Paris, and she followed him there. They travelled to Italy together, and she was always talking about getting married. But Edvard Munch felt certain that marriage was not for him. He had his paintings, that hardly left room for anything else – and with his poor health it would have been irresponsible of him to start a family. It would probably just lead to another home full of sick children. . .

89. The Dance of Life. Painting 1899.

90. The Death of Marat. Painting 1907.

Tulla came to visit him in Åsgårdstrand, and later Munch found he couldn't really remember how it had happened: there was a revolver in the house, and suddenly a shot rang out and a bullet ripped into one of the fingers of his left hand. This is how he recollected the drama, many years later:

He was holding the revolver in his hand, and Tulla said: 'What do you intend to do with that revolver?' He did not respond, holding the revolver in his firmly closed fist. 'Is it loaded?' He still did not respond, just stared into space without seeing anything. Munch got up, blood dripping from his hand. He looked around in confusion and lied down on the bed. Blood dripped from his left hand.

Suddenly he looked at Tulla with a cold expression in his eyes: 'You parasite. Don't let me bleed to death. Get a doctor!' For a long time he believed it was Tulla who had wanted to shoot him – he couldn't think of any other explanation. He became obsessed by the idea that she was actually a murderess.

So he took his revenge. He painted Tulla with a hideous look in her piercing eyes, standing full of triumph beside her victim after the deed was done. He painted as though in a fury, and used long broad sweeps of his brush – and as he worked it was as though a little of his anger evaporated.

91. Self Portrait with a Bottle of Wine. Painting 1906.

The years came and went in a whirl of excitement with travels, exhibitions, and work. The commissions poured in – so many people wanted him to do their portrait. Often he was too nervous to work – he had to drink a flask of red wine before he felt calm enough. For a while he lived in Germany with a rich doctor, in a beautiful house surrounded by a large park. It was like being a prince. He went about with counts and barons and had to wear evening dress or a frock coat. All his money worries were gone by now.

But there were other sorrows. Often he spent his evenings in cafés and restaurants feeling alone and friendless.

The drink became stronger, the attacks more frequent. He also felt prey to sudden bouts of anger, and he would start fighting with people.

92. *From Åsgårdstrand.*

93. *Edvard Munch painting in Åsgårdstrand.*

94. Girls on the Jetty. painting ca. 1900.

He thought always of Åsgårdstrand, of the white houses sleeping so peacefully between the trees. In his mind he planned the summer there – Inger would plant redcurrant and blackcurrant bushes there, and everything would be peaceful. But it didn't turn out that way. Instead there was drinking and parties, and he even got into a fistfight with another painter. It seemed to him that he had to get away from places where he might risk meeting people he knew from Kristiania. He had a vague feeling that they might be plotting against him.

95. Two Girls with blue Pinafores. Painting 1904/05.

But it was his own thoughts he wanted to get away from too. He no longer wanted to paint fear and death and jealousy, or even love. It had to be something outside his own mind – nature, little children, something uncorrupted and real. He wanted to get away from using gloomy colours too and use clear, strong colours instead. He painted his neighbours children in front of a yellow

96. Men Bathing. Painting 1907.

house in Åsgårdstrand and was delighted by the strong, bright colours.

But above all he wanted to get his nerves in good shape. In Germany he rented a fisherman's cottage by the sea. He felt the sea-air doing him good, it was almost like Åsgårdstrand. He got hold of a wonderful housekeeper who cooked his meals and organised things for him. So he went out in the bright sunlight and painted naked men on the beach. It was as though the sight of those healthy bodies emerging from a refreshing dip in the sea revitalised him.

But still his nerves were bad. He felt so uneasy all the time inside himself. He became afraid of meeting people, afraid to go out. One morning his legs wouldn't hold him any more, and the feeling was gone from his hand. He felt that he was on the verge of cracking up.

There were times when he felt almost mad, and he found himself a staring streight into the hideous face of insanity

He felt that something *had* to be done.

97. Dr. Jacobson is treating Edvard Munch in the clinic with passing electricity through his body. Drawing 1908/09.

A clinic for the nervously ill just outside Copenhagen was what saved him. He was given a strong medicine here that put him to sleep for eight days before the proper treatment began.

He was bathed and given a massage every day, and also a strange form of electrical treatment. He had to wrap up well and sit in front of an open window for hours, and it was so odd to be ordered about: 'Time to get up now, Mr Munch' 'Time for your walk now, Mr Munch' – that's the way they did things in those days.

He painted the head doctor, Dr Jacobson;because when he painted he was the one who had the power, he was the one who controlled the self-assured doctor. It seemed to him that his life was like a murky glass of water – he had to let it stand for a while, let the sediment settle on the bottom – get rid of his painful thoughts and all the unhappy memories. He began to make plans to live a quiet, withdrawn life. 'The alcohol-filled days of pain and happiness are finally over for me; . . . I am beginning to see the resemblence between women and flowers; I enjoy the scent of the blooms, but I never touch them and so I am never disappointed', he wrote to a friend.

He remained at the clinic for a whole winter, and while he was there he heard from Norway that he had been given his country's highest honour: for his services to art he had been awarded the Order of St Olaf.

98. Professor Daniel Jacobson. Painting 1909.

99. Self-portrait at the Clinic. Painting 1909.

100. Animals in the Zoo in Copenhagen. Lithograph 1909.

101. Galloping Horse. Painting 1910/12.

HOME TO NORWAY

102. From Kragerø.

Edvard Munch began to long to see the Norwegian countryside again. Of one thing he was quite sure – he did not want to go back to Kristiania again. He would live in a world not yet spoiled by human beings. He left Copenhagen and took the ferry along the southern coast of Norway. When the boat came in to Kragerø and he saw the little terraced town perched above the sea, his mind was made up. He would settle here. He found almost at once a large vacant house with a garden with tall trees and a view out over the sea. In his enthusiasm he found himself moved to deliver a short speech:'I am like Jonas, that was cast out from the belly of the whale and found himself on land. And I looked around and I saw that the land was good. 'The only listener, his cousin Ludvig Ravensberg, applauded warmly.

Cousin Ludvig was a great help at this time. He came to an arrangement with the best cook in town, and also employed two former seamen, Børre and Ellef. They were company for him, and did odd jobs about the place. Munch had a large open-air studio built in the garden, and then the work could commence. He didn't have to look far for his subject matter – all he had to do was look out the window or take a few steps outside in the garden and he had the most wonderful view stretching out before him.

He painted the worthy old pine tree that seemed to grow straight out of the rocks, and he felt himself as strong and peaceful as the tree and the nature that surrounded it.

103. Winter in Kragerø. Painting 1912.

104. Edvard Munch painting in Kragerø.

But a more important task awaited him. He had made up his mind to enter a competition to decorate the Aula, the newly built ceremonial hall at the university. Finally, after many difficulties, he was given the job.

He thought of what the university stood for – History and Research – the past and the future. There were three large spaces to be painted. On one he painted History such as he had experienced it at home while his father read aloud to the children – as a living communication between old and young.

He used the fisherman Børre as the model for the old man, and he painted him just as he really was, a bearded old sage in worn clothes. The cook's grandson was more than willing to pose as the young boy.

Munch painted the two of them under an enormous oak tree, of which there were a great many in Kragerø in those days. The landscape he placed them in were the bare and rocky hills that he could see from his window.

'History shows a distant and historically emotive landscape, in which an old man from the fjords, who has spent a life of hard toil, now sits sharing his rich storehouse of memories with an eagerly listening young boy', Munch explained.

People started to critizise his use of colours. 'Blue stones – those you can never find', they said. 'I have seen a lot of blue stones – and anyway, a horse can be red, yellow, white and blue, depending on how the light strikes it', Munch replied.

105. History. Lithograph 1914.

106. Edvard Munch with the painting 'History' in the open air studio in Kragerø.

107. Edvard Munch in his house in Kragerø.

108 The Researchers. (Once considered for use as he main section of the right wall in the University Aula) Painting 1912.

109. Edvard Munch with the painting "The Researchers" in the open air studio in Hvitsten.

In the next space he wanted to paint Research. Research means the future, and the best way to depict that was to paint a young mother breastfeeding her little child, Munch thougt. Surrounding her he painted older children, all of them busily studying and examining the flowers and stones, the insects and all of creation.

He needed a new studio for his big paintings, and to give himself more space he acquired another big house at Hvisten, on the other side of the Oslo fjord. The nature here was milder and the contours more gentle, and he thought it made a more fitting background for the figure of the mother.

When painting the mother with the baby, he remembered that long ago up in Hedmark, he had made a drawing of a peasant woman with a child. It was this image that gave him the idea of the Alma Mater.

Actually he was never completely happy about this picture – he did another version and made some slight changes to the group of trees and a few alterations to the children – but he never did manage to get it just as he wanted it.

Long after the University decorations were finished, he continued working on Alma Mater. He was never completely satisfied with it, and was always in two minds as to how its theme should be developed. Right up to his death he remained incertain as to whether that picture of the one calles 'The Researchers' should occupy the main place of honour in the Univerity hall.

It was lovely at Hvitsten. The woods were full of anemones and there was plenty of room for the chickens and turkeys he bought, so that he could keep himself in eggs and meat. In the summer there was plenty of activity on the beach below the house, and it cheered him up to see all the naked bodies swimming and lolling in the sun.

But people always seem to be critizising. They wanted the place as a public bathing place. 'What is more important, I ask, that your children should bathe, or that Alma Mater's children should?' Munch said.

110. Hihg Summer. Painting 1915.

111.The Sun. Painting 1912.

But he had to return to Kragerø to finish work on the Aula decorations. On the central wall of the hall, above the platform, there was to be a large painting. When people entered the room, this was the first thing they would see, and as they sat listening to the speeches or the music it was here their eyes would rest.

He thought for a long while about this picture, and tried out several different ideas. And then suddenly he had it – he would paint the sun as he saw it from the house at Kragerø, rising from the sea in the east.

From the house there's a little grass slope that leads down to the sea, with rocky hills to either side, then there's the belt of tiny rocky islands and beyond them the wide open sea. Early one morning he walked down there and saw the sun rise. He felt the warmth of the sunbeams and knew that this was the effect he wanted to achieve in his picture.

He never went near Kristiania all this time. Just the thought of all the people there was enough to put him in a bad mood. But once he paid a quick trip to town to look at a few of his old haunts.

112. The Dog 'Muff'. Painting ca. 1913.

113. Edvard Munch's horse 'Rousseau'.

114. Edvard Munch with the dog "Boy" at Jeløya.

In Pile Street, where he had lived as a child, nothing had changed – there was even a withered old Christmas tree out in the yard, just like there always used to be.

Some of his old restlessness returned, and he bought a new house, this time on Jeløya. Now he had three places where he could live and work. And every now and then he had a big prestigious exhibition in some foreign country.

His closest companions were the animals. The older he grew the less it seemed to him that there was much difference between humans and animals. His horse Rousseau had been with him since Kragerø, and now Rousseau too enjoyed the peaceful life at Jeløya. His dog Muff was more sociable than he was, and sometimes Munch had to take Muff with him to the cinema to keep him happy. The dog had his own ticket, and if he didn't think much of the film he wasn't afraid to let people know.

The First World War came, and the whole of Europe turned into a slaughter house. It was time now really to settle down. Ekely was for sale, and Munch enjoyed the thought of settling there and knowing he would live there for the rest of his life. Later he had a huge studio built, with plenty of room for big pictures. He would need that if he ever got another big commission for a job like the Aula decorations.

115. The Red House and Pine Trees. Painting 1935.

Now and then he made a quick trip into town to see an exhibition or visit some of his old stamping grounds. He visited Grünerløkka, but got a bit mixed up about the various places where he once lived. He remembered well enough the big red room where Inger gave her first piano lessons, and the little blue room where he had his first attack of rheumatic fever. . .

But soon he had to get back to his easel again. It wasn't that he felt compelled to paint all the time and always to have a brush in his hand – in fact, he didn't do much painting at this time. Most of the time he spent waiting for the desire to paint to come over him. It could break over him suddenly, like a wave, and he had to be close to home then and ready to start work at once. His friends probably thought it was odd that he didn't visit them more often, but then that was just how it was, and there was nothing to be done about it. He didn't even spend Christmas with his family, and he got the gardener to cut the top off a spruce tree and put it up in the living room. He thought it looked lovely even without decorations on it. And his brushes lay close by, ready for use.

116. The Artist and his Model. Painting ca. 1920.

117. Edvard Munch in his open air studio at Ekely.

118. Self-portrait at the Window. painting ca. 1940.

What he liked best was to be with just one person at a time. In that way he could do all the talking himself and prevent any disturbing thoughts from entering his head. Women came to the house, young and healthy. He painted them, and it made him feel old. There were other visitors, some who wanted to buy pictures, some who came just out of curiosity. He got the dogs to see most of them off.

Loneliness was his natural state. It always had been. He had no other offspring but his paintings, and he needed to have them round him in order to work, for work was life itself. There was so much talk about what art really was – but the answer was really quite simple. Art comes from one person's desire to open his heart to others, and that was what Munch had done.

119. Edvard Munch at Ekely on his 75 Birthday.

Biographical information

1863 Edvard Munch born on 12th December at Engelhaug, Loten in Hedmark, the son of army doctir Christian Munch and Laura Cathrine, nee Bjolstad.
1864 The family moves to Kristiania. 1868 His mother dies and her sister, Karen Bjolstad, takes over as mother to the children.
1877 His sister Sophie dies aged 15.
1879 Evard Munch enrolls at the Technical School.
1880 Leaves the Technical School in November and decides to become a painter.
1881 Starts at the School of Drawing in August.
1882 With 6 others he rents a studio in Stortings Place. Some instruction from Christian Krohg.
1883 Exhibits for the first time. Visits Frits Thaulow's open-air school in Modum.
1884 With Hans Jaeger and the bohemian set.
1885 Starts work on 'The Sick Child'
1886 Four paintings in the Autumn Exhibition, including 'The Sick Child'
1889 His first one-man show in April. In the summer he rents a house in Asgardstrand. Receives a state scholarship of 1500 kroner. In October he goes to Paris. Death of his father.
1890 Home in May. Summer in Asgardstrand and Kristiania. Receives second state scholarship, travels to France in November.
1891 In Nice and Paris. Summer in Norway. Receives state scholarship for the third time. Copenhagen and Paris in the autumn.
1892 Back to Norway at the end of March. Exhibits in Kristiania. Is invited to exhibit in Berlin. The show is closed after one week.
1893 In Berlin and meets, among others, August Strindberg. Paintings include 'Scream' and 'Madonna'.
1894 First etchings and lithographs printed in Berlin. Exhibition in Stockholm.
1895 I Paris and Berlin. Death of his brother Andreas.
1896 In Paris until Febuary. Contributes to shows. Prints coloured lithographs and makes his first woodcuts.
1897 In July goes to Asgardstrand where he buys a house. Exhibition in Kristiania in September.
1898 To Berlin in March. Paris in May. June in Kristiania. he meets Tulla Larsen.
1899 Travels to Berlin, Paris, Nice, Firenze, Rome. The autumn and winter are spent at the Kornhaug Sanatorium in Gudbrandsdalen.
1900 To Berlin in March, Firenze, Rome and on to a sanatorium in Switzerland. Painta 'The Dance of Life'.
1902 Winter and spring in Berlin. Exhibits 'The Frieze of Life' in Berlin. Summer in Asgardstrand. Shoots himself in the left hand.
1903 In Berlin and Paris.
1904 In Berlin. March and April in Weimar. Summer in Asgardstrand.
1905 The exhibnition in Prague is one of the greatest successes of his career. Travels to Bad Elgersburg in Thuringen suffering from alcoholism and nerve problems.
1906 To Weimar, where he is presented at court.
1907 Winter in Berlin. Summer and autumn in Warnemunde.
1908 Winter in Berlin. Summer in Warnemunde. He experiences a nervous breakdown in Copenhagen and admits himself to Dr Jacobsen's nerve clinic. Receives the Royal Norwegian Orderof St Olaf.
1909 Winter and spring at Dr Jacobsen's clinic. Home to Norway in May. Settles at Kragero. Begins work on the murals at Oslo University.
1910 Buys the property Ramme at Hvitsten. Continues working on the murals.
1912 His own room at the exhibition in Cologne.
1913 Rents Grimsrod, a large estate on Jeloya. Is feted on the occasion of his 50th birthday.
1914 To Berlin and Paris. After many years discussion and conflict the University finally accepts the Aula murals.
1916 Buys the property Ekely in Skoyen, where he spends the rest of his life. Unveiling of the Aula murals on 19th September.
1919 Suffers a bout of Spanish flue.
1920–21 Visits Berlin and Paris.
1922 To Berlin and Zurich. Murals for the Freia Chocolate Factory, the 'Freia frieze'.
1927 To Berliln, Munich, Rome, Firenze and Dresden. Large exhibitions in Berlin and Oslo.
1928 Works on outlines for the decoration of Oslo Town Hall.
1933 Receives the Great Cross of St Olaf as part of the celebrations of his 70th birthday.
1940 Norway occupied by the German invaders. Munch has no contact with the Nazis, either German or Norwegian.
1943 Celebrations on his 80th birthday.
1944 Dies quietly at Ekely, 23rd January. All work in his possession at the time of his death is left to Oslo city.